James Cross Giblin

MILK
THE FIGHT FOR PURITY

Illustrated with Photographs and Prints

Thomas Y. Crowell   New York

Also by James Cross Giblin

The Truth About Santa Claus
Chimney Sweeps: Yesterday and Today
The Skyscraper Book

Library of Congress Cataloging-in-Publication Data
Giblin, James.
    Milk: the fight for purity.

    Summary: Traces the history of the centuries-long
effort of philanthropists, scientists, and consumers
to make milk a reliably pure and safe product.
    1. Milk hygiene—History—Juvenile literature.
2. Milk as food—History—Juvenile literature.
3. Dairying—History—Juvenile literature.   4. Milk
hygiene—United States—History—Juvenile literature.
5. Milk as food—United States—History—Juvenile
literature.   6. Dairying—United States—History—
Juvenile literature.   [1. Milk.   2. Milk hygiene.
3. Dairying]   I. Title.
SF257. G53 1986   637.1   85-48252
ISBN 0-690-04572-7
ISBN 0-690-04574-3 (lib. bdg.)

For my mother, Anna Cross Giblin, with love

ACKNOWLEDGMENTS

For their help in providing research material and illustrations, the author thanks the following individuals and institutions:

Agricultural Marketing Service, U.S. Department of Agriculture; Sue Alexander; Atlantic Dairy Association; Joan W. Blos; Borden Inc.; The Central Park Conservancy; Committee for a Sane Nuclear Policy; *Detroit Free Press;* William B. Hastings; Department of Health and Human Services, Public Health Service, Food and Drug Administration; International Association of Milk, Food and Environmental Sanitarians, Inc.; Henry W. Jeffers III, Walker-Gordon Laboratory Company; The Library of Congress; Murray Liebman; The Metropolitan Museum of Art; Jim Murphy; Museum of the City of New York; National Dairy Council; The New-York Historical Society, New York City; The New York Public Library; Lila Perl; Jeanne Prahl; Ruth Price, Photography Division, U.S. Department of Agriculture; Peg Rivers; Robert Sanders, Milk Safety Branch, Food and Drug Administration; Swarthmore College Peace Collection; Jane Resh Thomas

CONTENTS

1

Perfect Food or Poison?

Milk, smooth and white and sweet tasting, is the first food most of us know by name. Every human baby lives for a time on nothing but milk, obtained either from its mother's breasts or a bottle.

Older children and adults drink a lot of milk, too. In many homes, the refrigerator is never without a large carton or container of milk. And who doesn't remember a parent nagging now and then, "Finish your glass of milk, dear"?

Given these facts, it should come as no surprise to learn that milk is the most widely consumed food in the United States today. In 1981, the average American drank almost one hundred quarts of milk.

There are several good reasons for milk's popularity. One is that it has long been considered "the most nearly perfect food." It earned that title because it is easily digested by most babies, children, and many adults, and because it contains so many different nutrients.

1

A glass of milk.

COURTESY OF U.S. DEPARTMENT OF AGRICULTURE

Cow's milk is usually composed of the following solids: lactose sugar (4.9%); fat (4%); protein (3.55%); and minerals (0.75%). Milk is also rich in vitamins, especially vitamins A, D, E, and K. The rest of the milk, about 87%, is water.

The sugar and fat in milk help to supply the heat and energy the body needs. Milk protein builds and maintains body tissues and aids in forming antibodies that fight infection. The minerals in milk, chiefly calcium, play an important part in the development of strong bones and teeth. In 1980 it was estimated that 72% of the calcium available in the U.S. food supply was provided by milk and milk products.

Most people today take a supply of pure milk for granted. Unless there's a strike of milk processors or deliverers, shoppers expect to find the dairy section of their favorite store filled with cartons of cool, fresh milk. If they're worried about their weight, chances are they'll pass by the cartons of whole milk and select the low-fat or skim variety instead. But whatever type of milk they choose, they will probably have no worries about whether it's safe to drink.

That wasn't always the case. Less than one hundred years ago there were some who called milk "white poison" because of the deadly bacteria that were often found in it. More recently, sales of milk were stopped in some places in the United States because people feared that the liquid contained dangerous levels of radioactivity.

In the last few decades, there's been much talk in the United States and other countries about the need for consumer protection. Writers have revealed the dangers of faulty appliances and unsafe motor vehicles. Scientists have exposed the health hazards caused by the use of chemical additives in foods.

Long before these issues came to public attention, however, another battle for consumer protection was already under way. It was the struggle to ensure a safe, reliable supply of milk for the world's children and adults. This book tells the story of that struggle and the men and women who have taken part in it. The struggle began almost as soon as people started to drink the milk of cows and other animals. And it is still going on today.

2

Cows in the City

Milk and dairy products have been part of the human diet ever since people in the Middle East first tamed wild cattle nine or ten thousand years ago.

The world's earliest written records, found in India and dating back nearly six thousand years, mention milk as being an essential food. A five-thousand-year-old wall painting from the Babylonian city of Ur shows dairy workers milking cows and straining the fresh milk into large jars. The Bible describes Canaan as "a land flowing with milk and honey."

Not everyone in the ancient world consumed milk products, however. In order to digest the lactose sugar in milk, people have to produce an enzyme called lactase in their stomachs. Babies produce this enzyme readily, but children lose the ability after they are weaned from their mothers, or by the age of six, unless they continue to drink milk and eat butter and cheese.

In the Middle East, where people often moved from

place to place, they depended on their herds of cattle to provide them with much of their food. These people continued to drink milk and to produce lactase as they grew to maturity. But the people of China, Japan, and other parts of Asia, Africa, and the Americas did not domesticate cattle. As a result, they ceased to produce lactase in their bodies and suffered from stomach cramps, vomiting, and diarrhea if they tried to drink milk. Because of this, many Chinese in ancient times believed that all animal milk must be unclean.

In the Western world, the consumption of milk spread from the Middle East to Egypt and the Roman Empire. Egyptian and Roman recipes for bread and cakes included milk as one of the chief ingredients.

When the Romans colonized Western Europe, they brought herds of cattle with them. Later, in the fifth century A.D., Europe was overrun by a number of nomadic tribes—among them the Goths, Vandals, and Franks—who defeated the mighty Roman armies. These tribes lived mainly on the milk, cheese, and meat they obtained from their animals. In fact, one of their main reasons for moving into Europe from the east was to find new grazing lands for their herds.

After the roving tribes settled down, the raising of animals for milk and meat continued to be one of the chief activities of European agriculture. Cattle weren't the only animals involved. Sheep's milk was used to make cheese in southern Europe; people drank goat's milk in countries along the Mediterranean; and the people of the far north milked herds of reindeer.

Cow's milk was by far the most popular, though. One English writer of the Middle Ages said that every English farmer needed at least enough grazing land to keep a cow. For only a cow could provide the "butter, cheese, cream, sweet milk, sour milk, and buttermilk" that were already so important to the English diet.

The milker. Engraving after a painting by the Dutch artist Lucas van Leyden (1494–1533).

In the Middle Ages, farmers in England and Europe were still raising cattle in much the same way that farmers had been doing for hundreds of years. Every morning they milked their cows in the barn or shed, and then led them out to pasture. In the evening they brought the animals in from the fields and milked them again.

Not all female dairy cattle could be milked. As with humans, cows cannot produce any milk until their first offspring is born. A cow usually bears her first calf when she is two years old, and is milked for ten months after giving birth. Then she is allowed to "dry off" until her next calf is born. Most cows are milked for about seven years.

The cows of the Middle Ages produced plenty of milk in the summer months, when the fields were covered with thick grass and clover. But they gave little in the winter, especially in the north. Most farmers did not grow and store hay for fodder, so the animals became scrawny when frost withered the grasses and snow covered the earth. During January and February, many of the weaker cows sickened and died.

When spring came, the surviving animals soon grew sleek and fat, and milk yields were high once more. Since there was no refrigeration at the time, most of the milk was made into butter and cheese. These could be stored

Young herdsmen with cows. Painting by the Dutch artist Aelbert Cuyp (1620–1691).

on the farm for future use or sold in the nearby town or village marketplace.

Few people, even children, drank fresh milk, since it turned sour so quickly, especially on hot summer days. Cooks used fresh milk in cooking and baking, though, and rich cream poured over fruit or a pudding was a special treat.

Farmers who lived near a large city like London often drove a cow or two through the streets early in the morning. "Ho! Milk here!" a farmer would call, and housewives or servant girls would come out of their houses carrying pails and jars. Then the farmer would milk one of the cows into the pail while the customer watched. He did his best to keep his animals healthy and clean; otherwise, the customer might wait to buy until a better-looking cow came along.

As cities grew bigger, some farmers began to keep herds of cattle on large fields or commons within their boundaries. In London, Hampstead Heath, Lincoln's Inn Fields, and St. James's Park all provided pasturage for cows. The animals were tended by milkmaids, who also delivered milk throughout the city. A young woman would carry the milk in two pails hanging from a yoke across her shoulders. Unfortunately the pails were left uncovered, so the milk was open to whatever might fall into it from the sky.

My rest you'd disturb early in the morn
Leave me in bed comfortless and forlorn
Milk and water will not with me agree.
Therefore I'll nothing have to do with thee.

Milkmaid in a London street. Eighteenth-century English print.

Housewives often discovered specks of soot or small twigs in the milk they bought from milkmaids, and wondered if the milk was safe to use. But there wasn't much they could do about it, given the lack of sanitary standards at the time.

When the English, French, Dutch, and Spanish began to explore North America in the 1500s and 1600s, they found no native cattle in the new territories. The settlers who followed had to bring their own animals with them. The Pilgrims of Plymouth received their first cattle in 1624, when a ship from England brought them three young cows and a bull. Dutch colonists arrived in New Amsterdam in 1624 aboard a fleet of ships that also carried horses, sheep, pigs, and a herd of Holstein cows.

The Dutch were noted for the good care they gave their animals. In 1625, they shipped 103 cows to New Amsterdam aboard one vessel. For safety's and comfort's sake, each animal was provided with a separate stall, the floor of which was covered with three feet of sand. The sand helped to make waste removal easier during the long ocean voyage. As a result of such treatment, all but two of the cows survived the trip in excellent condition.

In the west, Spanish colonists from Mexico brought cattle with them when they founded San Diego, California, in 1769. Herds of cattle also accompanied the

Franciscan monks who built mission churches in California as far north as San Francisco. A severe famine struck California between 1772 and 1774, and one of the monks wrote in his diary that often he and his brothers "had only the grass from our fields and the milk from our cows to live on."

The American colonists, like their relatives in Europe, had no mechanical means of refrigeration, so they had to find other ways of keeping milk fresh. Pails full of milk and cream were dropped down into deep, cool wells until they were used. Where it was possible, a special dairy house might be built over an existing stream on a farm. The water running beneath the springhouse would chill the milk and help to keep it from turning sour.

As American cities grew in the 1700s, people often pastured their animals on land set aside for that purpose in the heart of town. The Boston Common, like many of the parks in London, became well-known as a pasture for cattle. In New York City, the barrier along Wall Street prevented cows from wandering out of the common pasture in Battery Park.

By the early 1800s, cities in America and Europe were growing bigger all the time. As their populations increased, so did the demand for milk. The herds in the common pastures couldn't produce enough to satisfy that demand. Besides, the land they occupied was needed for new homes, stores, office buildings, and parks for people. Gradually city dwellers stopped keeping cows and sold their animals to farmers in the surrounding countryside.

While this was going on, a new type of businessman—the milk seller—made his appearance in the streets of New York, Boston, Philadelphia, and other large cities. Sometimes the milk seller was a farmer from an outlying suburb who owned a large herd of cows and sold his own milk. More often he was a city merchant to whom small farmers brought their milk for distribution.

A New York City milk seller of 1840. Watercolor by Nicolino Calyo (1799–1884).

Some milk sellers carried their milk supply in buckets suspended from yokes across their shoulders, like the milkmaids of London. Others sold their milk from the backs of horse-drawn wagons. The milk delivered by wagon was usually contained in large metal cans. Sometimes the cans had lids, sometimes not.

As the seller walked or rode through the streets, he would often call, "Milk come! Milk come!" Then he might go on to chant:

> *"Here's new milk from the cow,*
> *Which is so nice and so fine,*
> *That the doctors do say*
> *It is much better than wine."*

When a housewife heard the seller's call, she would come out into the street with a pitcher or pail, and the seller would fill it from one of his cans. He used a quart measure so that he'd know how much to charge. In the 1830s, milk sold in New York City and other American cities for four to six cents a quart.

Milk sellers also roamed the streets of London, where they had replaced the milkmaids of earlier times. Many of their customers looked on the sellers with suspicion. They claimed that the men possessed "neither character, nor decency of manner, nor cleanliness."

Some Londoners accused the milk sellers of an even more serious offense. They charged that much of the sellers' milk came from a "black cow." That was their name for the black water pumps under which they said the sellers thinned the milk in order to increase their profits. If a pump wasn't handy, they claimed, some sellers watered their milk from horse troughs.

Watering of milk was widespread in American cities, too. Before setting out on their morning deliveries, many sellers would fill their cans only three quarters full of milk and then add water at the top. This practice was so common that a popular verse of the day went:

> *A quart of Milk, good man, I'll take*
> *'Tis for my little dark-eyed daughter,—*
> *But tell me, sir, for her sweet sake*
> *Ah! tell me 'tis not Milk and Water!*

Many people were upset by this situation, but there seemed to be little they could do to improve it. No American city yet had any laws regulating the distribution and sale of milk. There weren't even any commonly accepted standards as to how much liquid and solids a quart of milk should contain.

All that was soon to change. For people were about to discover a new health hazard involving milk, one far more serious than watering.

3

Swill Milk

From a distance, the small New York City factory of the 1830s looks like a collection of ramshackle wooden sheds with tall brick chimneys that belch black smoke. Any number of things might be manufactured inside the sheds—barrels, plows, wagon wheels. Only the strong smell surrounding the place reveals that it is, in fact, a distillery where corn and rye are made into whiskey.

Something else clearly identifies the establishment as a distillery of the time: the sound of cattle lowing in one of the larger sheds. For distillers had discovered that dairying could be a profitable sideline occupation. All they had to do was buy a herd of cows, build a stable for them next to the distillery, and feed them on the swill left over after the whiskey had been distilled.

Huge carts delivered fresh supplies of corn and rye to the distilleries each day. They were ground at the rate of a hundred bushels an hour and the alcohol was extracted. Then the slop, which contained water from the distilling process, ran off into large wooden storage tanks. From there it was conveyed through elevated pipes to the stable next door.

The cattle stood in rows of seven to ten across the building. Most of their stalls were no more than three feet wide by eleven feet long. Some New York City dairies of the 1830s were still surrounded by open fields, in which the cows could graze and get some exercise. But most of the cows in the swill-milk dairies never left their stalls from the time they entered them.

Stablehands in a distillery dairy. Sketch from FRANK LESLIE'S ILLUSTRATED NEWSPAPER.

An average cow in one of the dairies consumed about thirty-two gallons of swill a day. The animals drank no fresh water, since the distillers figured they were getting enough water from the swill. Nor were most of them given any hay or other solid fodder to eat. As a result their teeth soon began to go bad because they had nothing to chew on.

Although the animals were weak, unfit specimens, they were milked daily, and their product was distributed to unsuspecting customers throughout New York City.

In 1842 a foe of alcoholic beverages, Robert Hartley, wrote an exposé of the swill-milk business. He revealed that swill milk was being sold in a number of American cities including Boston, Philadelphia, and Cincinnati. The center of the industry was New York City, where over five hundred swill-milk dairies were located, each containing an average of twenty cows. These cows produced more than five million gallons of swill milk each year.

Hartley described the milk as being "very thin and of a pale bluish color." To make it look richer and whiter, he claimed that the distillery dairymen frequently added starch, flour, plaster of Paris, and chalk. In some of the dairies the mixing was done in unclean cans, and the milkmen who handled the job were dirty also.

Because of this, Hartley suggested, there might well

be a connection between swill milk and the startling rise in infant deaths. In 1815, children under five had represented 33% of the deaths in Boston, 32% of the deaths in New York, and 25% of the deaths in Philadelphia. By 1839, infant deaths accounted for almost 50% of the mortality rate in New York and Philadelphia, and 43% of the rate in Boston. Hartley charged that this increase was at least partly due to the fact that children were drinking impure swill milk.

Many people were concerned about Hartley's disclosures, and in 1848 the New York Academy of Medicine appointed a committee to investigate swill milk. The members found that most of the milk they sampled had far less nutritional value than regular milk. For example, a thousand parts of pure milk from an upstate New York county contained about thirty-five parts of butterfat, while the same amount of swill milk contained less than fifteen parts of butterfat.

The committee summed up its findings by declaring that swill milk was "positively detrimental, especially to young children, and is a probable cause of many fatal diseases." However, the committee made no mention of the large number of tiny organisms called bacteria that swill milk contained. In the 1840s most people still did not know that diseases were caused by harmful bacteria.

Unfortunately no laws were passed to regulate or

outlaw swill milk in the wake of the committee's report. The distillery dairymen managed to persuade their friends in city government that the problem was not nearly as serious as Hartley and the committee had implied. Meanwhile the mortality rate among children in New York and other cities continued to rise.

The spread of railroad lines in the late 1840s opened a new source of milk for city residents. For the first time, country milk from farms as far as seventy miles away could be transported by train to city milk depots. There dealers picked up the milk, for delivery by horse and wagon to individual consumers.

Shipment by railroad had its drawbacks, however. The milk cans rode in ordinary baggage or box cars. There was no refrigeration in the cars, and much of the milk often turned sour during the three- or four-hour journey, especially in summer.

The cost of shipping, added to the cost of the milk itself, also made country milk more expensive than milk from distillery dairies. Wealthy people gladly paid the higher price in order to obtain pure milk, but poor people had to settle for the cheaper swill milk.

In the 1850s another alternative to swill milk came to public notice. This was condensed milk, developed by the inventor Gail Borden. Borden got the idea for condensed milk during a rough voyage across the

PURE & WHOLESOME MILK,

JAMAICA MILK DAIRY.

The inhabitants of NEW-YORK and BROOKLYN are respectfully informed, that an extensive Dairy, for the supply of PURE MILK, has been recently established as above. The cows are fed upon the most nutritious grasses, meal, and roots, without any addition whatever of *distillery slops*, or any other unwholsome food ; and the utmost care and vigilance will be exercised for the delivery, at the dwellings of subscribers, of the milk fresh and unadulterated.

Every arrangement which can in any degree promote the health of the animals, and the supply of wholesome, cleanly, and rich milk, has been made ; and the establishment is with confidence submitted for the patronage of families, and especially of parents.

Families will be punctually supplied, at their residences, at *six cents a quart*, by leaving their names with the several distributors, or at the office in New-York, at No. 225 Pearl-street, (entrance on Platt-street.) Boxes, for the reception of orders or complaints, are placed at the stores of Messrs. W. B. Windle & Son, No. 56 Maiden-lane, and No. 597 Broadway, at the office of the New-York Observer, No. 142 Nassau-street, at Messrs. Tracy, Gould & Co.'s, No. 27 Wall-street, at the office of the Greenwich Insurance Company, No. 306 Hudson-street, and at the Fulton and South Ferry Houses, Brooklyn.　　　　　　　　July 11, 1840.

Advertisements like this promised city customers pure, fresh milk from the country.

Atlantic in 1851 when he was returning home from a trip to England. Two cows were stabled in the hold of the ship to provide fresh milk for the infants on board. The ship rocked so much, though, that the cows became seasick and couldn't be milked. As a result, several of the infants died before the ship reached New York.

Saddened by this tragedy, Borden wondered if there wasn't some way to condense and store milk so that such a terrible thing could never happen in the future. He began to experiment with milk, seeking a new way of preserving it.

Borden knew that the Shakers used a vacuum pan to preserve fruits, so he moved to a Shaker community in New Lebanon, New York, to work with their equipment. By 1853 he had developed a pure, fresh milk with most of the water removed in a vacuum pan at low temperature. The vacuum container assured that there would be no contamination from the air, and the drying method retained the color and flavor of the milk.

Borden called the new product condensed milk. He added sugar to help preserve it, and packaged it for sale in hermetically sealed cans. Condensed milk could be kept almost indefinitely, and then mixed with water when used so that it would have the consistency of regular milk. One can of condensed milk, according to Borden's ads, made two and a half quarts of ordinary milk.

Borden insisted on strict standards in the dairies that supplied the fresh milk he used for manufacturing condensed milk. The cows' udders were washed thoroughly in warm water before milking. The barns were swept clean at least once a day. Everything in the dairies was painted white, and all the employees wore white gowns, caps, and gloves, like doctors.

Gail Borden (1801–1874).

Alononzo Holister, who worked with Gail Borden, is shown standing beside the vacuum pan in which Borden first successfully condensed milk. The pan is now at the Smithsonian Institution.

However, Borden had a hard time marketing his condensed milk at first. For one thing, like country milk it was more expensive than swill milk. For another, housewives had to be persuaded that milk from a can was superior to milk from a cow. Despite everything that had been written about the dangers of swill milk, they were suspicious of condensed milk and feared that it had been tampered with in some unwholesome way.

Condensed milk proved its worth during the American Civil War, 1861–65, when the federal government purchased thousands of cans to help feed Union soldiers at the front. After the war, more and more civilians began to use condensed milk in their homes, but it never replaced liquid milk in popularity. Nor did it solve the problem of milk safety, which remained as pressing as ever.

4

New Laws, New Problems

In 1855 New York, the nation's largest city, had a population of over 700,000. Its inhabitants spent more than six million dollars each year for milk. Of that, less than two million went for pure country milk. The rest, over four million dollars, was spent on swill milk from the distillery dairies. As a journalist of the day wrote, "The profits to be made from swill milk, and not the 'milk of human kindness,' have influenced the distillers to enlarge their herds."

More and more people began to link the consumption of swill milk with the startling rise in infant deaths in New York City. Between 1843 and 1856 the death rate of children under five in the city more than tripled. It was 13% higher than the infant mortality rate in London, which had some of the worst slums in the world.

Groups of concerned citizens joined forces to demand that something be done about the distillery dairies. Responding to the outcry, *Frank Leslie's Illustrated News-*

paper, one of the leading publications of the day, sent its reporters to investigate the most notorious dairies in New York and its sister city, Brooklyn.

"Swill milk should be branded with the word 'poison' just as narcotic drugs are," *Leslie's* said in May, 1858. Its reporters went on to describe the appalling conditions in one of the largest Brooklyn dairies. The stables were long wooden buildings with ceilings so low a person could reach up and touch them. Cobwebs hung thickly everywhere.

The stables housed hundreds of cows. They were tied in place when they were first purchased and seldom moved until they died or were sold to butchers. Three times a day boiling swill from the distillery's tanks came foaming down into their troughs. It was so hot that it sometimes scalded the animals' mouths.

On a hot summer day the temperature in the windowless stables often rose to 110° Fahrenheit. In the winter all openings in the walls were sealed so that the stables would remain hot and the cows could be milked as frequently as possible. The stables were rarely cleaned. Manure piled up in the stalls until it was finally loaded onto wagons and dumped into nearby creeks or streams.

Few cows survived more than six months in a distillery stable. Either they developed severe stomach problems from eating nothing but swill, or they contracted tuberculosis. When a cow became too weak to stand, she was

Milking a dying cow in a distillery dairy. Sketch from FRANK LESLIE'S ILLUSTRATED NEWSPAPER.

supported by ropes or a hoist and milked until she died. Then she was immediately replaced with another cow, so that the output of the dairy wouldn't be affected.

The milk from sick and dying cows was mixed with milk from healthy animals and sold throughout the city. To conceal the true nature of their product, swill-milk dealers hung signs saying "Pure Country Milk" or "Grass

Fed Milk" on the sides of their carts.

Children who drank swill milk often suffered from terrible diarrhea. Because they didn't get the nourishment they needed, they were more likely to fall victim to common childhood diseases like chicken pox and measles. Sometimes the children became so weakened from a combination of ailments that they died.

As a result of the articles in *Leslie's Weekly*, several dairy owners, fearing legal action, closed their stables completely. Others sold their diseased animals and cleaned

Loading milk from a distillery dairy on a cart marked "Pure Country Milk." Sketch from FRANK LESLIE'S ILLUSTRATED NEWSPAPER.

up their facilities. The mayor of New York, working with the Common Council of Brooklyn, appointed a committee to investigate conditions in the remaining stables. Most important of all, public opinion had been aroused, not only in New York but in other cities where distillery stables were located.

In 1862 New York State passed a law that forbade keeping cows in "crowded or unhealthy conditions" or feeding them food that produces "impure, diseased or unwholesome milk." The law also stated that the source of the milk had to be clearly marked on delivery carts. No longer could a swill-milk dealer claim that he sold "Pure Country Milk."

Massachusetts in 1864 outlawed the sale of milk obtained from cows fed on distillery waste or anything else that would affect the quality of the milk. The Massachusetts law also prohibited the sale of milk from diseased cows.

New York strengthened its existing law in 1864 by stating: "Any milk that is obtained from animals fed on distillery waste, usually called swill, is hereby declared to be impure and unwholesome." This effectively brought an end to swill dairies in the New York area.

In the next few years many other states, including Pennsylvania, Illinois, Kentucky, and Indiana, forbade the sale of milk from swill-fed cows. With these laws, one cause of the high infant mortality rate in the United States came under control at last.

Along with swill milk, public health officials were also troubled by the continuing adulteration of milk with water, baking soda, and chalk. Adulteration hit the poor the hardest. As a milk inspector in Boston said, "It is the poorest classes, who buy in small quantities, who receive the largest amount of adulteration. And they are the least able to contend with it." Even so-called "pure country milk" was sometimes adulterated before it reached the consumer.

At last, in 1864, the same Massachusetts law that forbade the sale of swill milk also prohibited the sale of milk adulterated with water or any other substance. New York had passed a law against the sale of adulterated milk in 1862 and made the law even stronger in 1864. Five years later, in 1869, Massachusetts toughened its law by stating that anyone found selling adulterated milk would be fined not less than twenty or more than one hundred dollars, large sums of money at the time.

Adding teeth to these new laws was the invention of a device called the lactometer, which accurately measured the solids contained in milk. By the early 1890s the accepted standard for milk quality in New York and many other states was 12% solids, of which 3% had to

31

be fat. If a test by a lactometer showed that milk contained fewer solids than that, the dealer would be subject to a fine or other punishment.

While city milk inspectors were paying closer atten-

THE CITY MILK BUSINESS.

MARY, THE KITCHEN-MAID. "Why, John, what's the matter?"
MILKMAN. "Ah, Mary! if we don't have rain soon, I don't know what we'll do for Milk!"

Delivering milk in the mid-1800s. The ash from the milkman's cigar is about to fall into the maid's pitcher. Sketch from FRANK LESLIE'S ILLUSTRATED NEWSPAPER.

tion to the content of milk, new developments were taking place in the way it was sold. Before the late 1870s, milk was still being dispensed to housewives from large metal cans on the backs of delivery wagons. People realized that this was an unsanitary practice, since dust and dirt could easily get into the cans. But no one knew what to do about the problem until 1878, when the idea for a milk bottle was patented by an inventor in Brooklyn, New York.

This first milk bottle was simply a jar with a glass top. Designs for other types of bottles followed, and in 1884 Dr. Henry G. Thatcher of Potsdam, New York, patented a design for a quart glass container with a top that could be tightly sealed.

Thatcher had felt compelled to invent a bottle after lining up one day in 1883 to buy some milk from a passing dealer. A little girl who was ahead of Thatcher in the line accidentally dropped her dirty rag doll into the open can of milk while the dealer was filling her pitcher. The man apparently thought nothing of it. He reached into the can, pulled out the doll, shook it off, and handed it back to the little girl. Then, smiling, he turned to serve Thatcher.

Some dairymen opposed the use of milk bottles, because there was a high rate of breakage and it cost more to handle them. The public liked the new bottles, though, and by the mid-1890s Thatcher's design had been adopted by dairies all across the country.

In a typical model dairy of the time, milk was received from nearby farmers as well as from the dairy's own herds. The milk was cooled on the second floor of the dairy in a 150-gallon vat with a box full of ice suspended inside.

When the milk's temperature fell to 50° F, it flowed through pipes to the floor below, where quart-size glass bottles were waiting in metal frames that held twenty bottles each. The dairy's workers filled the bottles by hand, sealed them, and stored them in vats of ice until it was time to ship them by wagon or railroad. After the empty bottles were returned to the dairy, they were washed in boiling water and used again.

Milk bottled in a dairy like this might be handled with the utmost care from the time the farmer milked the cow until the milk reached the people who drank it. It might meet all the accepted tests for fat and solids content. It might look absolutely pure and white.

By the 1890s, though, many people realized that the appearance of milk could be deceptive. Because of recent advances in science and medicine, they knew that seemingly pure milk might actually be a carrier of disease.

5

Milk and Disease

Long before the 1890s, doctors had suspected that impure milk might help to transmit such dread diseases as tuberculosis, typhoid fever, cholera, and scarlet fever. But they had no way to prove it.

As far back as 1683, a Dutch maker of microscopes, Anton van Leeuwenhoek, had reported seeing thousands of tiny, single-celled organisms moving about in samples of water and saliva. What Leeuwenhoek had observed under his microscope were bacteria, but it was close to two centuries before other scientists began to make a connection between bacteria and the spread of disease. Instead, many thought that epidemics broke out when people breathed in "miasmas"—mysterious vapors rising from the earth.

Not until the mid-1800s did the germ theory of disease replace such unscientific notions. By then scientists had confirmed that in every substance there were huge numbers of bacteria. Most of these bacteria were harmless, and many performed useful functions. But some bacteria, which scientists called germs, could cause disease when they entered the human body through the nostrils, mouth, or skin. A researcher named John Snow presented convincing evidence in 1854 that cholera was spread by germs in unclean water. Another scientist, William Budd, proved in 1873 that water-borne germs were also a cause of typhoid fever.

Milk was revealed to be a disease carrier when the German scientist, Robert Koch, discovered the bacteria that caused tuberculosis in 1882. Koch found that there were three types of tubercle bacteria, or bacilli, that affected people. The most common was spread from person to person, and destroyed the lungs if it was not controlled in time. The rarest was a type carried by infected birds. In between was yet another type that could be transmitted through the milk of diseased cattle.

Cattle, or bovine, tuberculosis struck the glands, intestines, and bones of its human victims. If it didn't kill them, it might leave them hunchbacked or physically deformed in some other way. Children seemed to be especially susceptible to bovine tuberculosis. When the disease affected their spines, children were sent to hospitals, where they often spent years strapped into spinal frames. The frames were designed to prevent deformity while the body slowly overcame the infection.

In 1887 Sir David Bruce, a medical officer in the

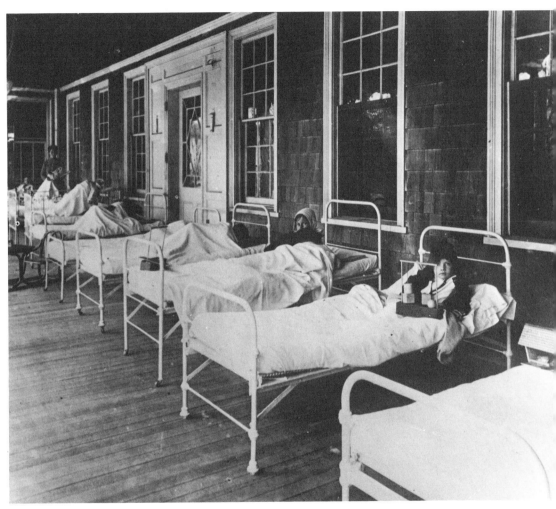

Children suffering from tuberculosis rest on the porch of a sanitarium in this photo taken in the 1880s. It was believed that cold, fresh air would help victims overcome the disease. Photo by Jacob A. Riis.

British army, isolated the bacteria of another serious disease that was spread by milk from infected cattle, sheep, and goats. The disease was named brucellosis, after its discoverer. Its symptoms were fever, chills, sweats, weakness, pain, and severe aches that could last for as long as six months.

For reasons not clearly understood, adults were more

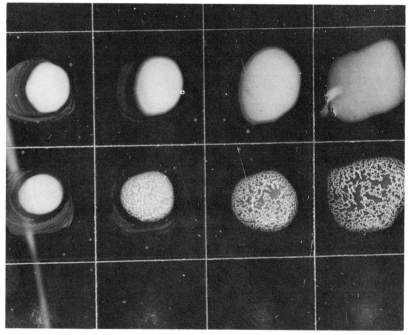

COURTESY OF U.S. DEPARTMENT OF AGRICULTURE

To test dairy cattle for brucellosis, a specially prepared suspension of brucella organisms is added to a sample of blood serum taken from a cow. If the cow has brucellosis, the organisms of the disease in her blood will join with those in the suspension and form clumps. The gradual appearance of such clumps can clearly be seen in the last three photos of this sequence.

likely to get brucellosis than children. Most victims of the disease recovered completely within six months, but some suffered from recurring attacks for the rest of their lives.

Nineteenth-century scientists discovered that other diseases could be transmitted to people via cow's milk even though the animal herself was perfectly healthy. If the cow's udder wasn't clean, bits of dung containing coliform bacteria might get into the milk. These bacteria often caused serious intestinal disorders. Or perhaps someone who was infected with a disease handled the milk on the farm or in a dairy. Outbreaks of typhoid fever, diphtheria, and scarlet fever were traced back to contamination of milk by humans.

Once it had been proved conclusively that milk could spread disease, people sought in various ways to stop this from happening.

In 1870 the U.S. Public Health Service had been organized as a national agency. Its purpose was to prevent disease, prolong human life, and promote health and hygiene. In 1887, responding to advances in the study of bacteria, the Public Health Service established a laboratory to study the causes of disease in the United States, including impure milk.

A new way to control bovine tuberculosis appeared on the scene in 1890, when Robert Koch accidentally discovered a test for the disease. Koch, who had isolated the tubercle bacillus in 1882, was trying to perfect a vaccine that would produce immunity against the disease in cattle. His vaccine did not work on experimental cows, but Koch observed that a strange swelling occurred at the point of injection in some animals.

Koch pursued his experiments and found that the cattle that developed the swelling were already suffering from tuberculosis. Thus Koch's vaccine, although it failed to serve its intended purpose, proved to have an unexpected value. It helped to identify cows that were infected with tuberculosis even when they seemed to be completely healthy.

Koch's injection, which came to be known as the tuberculin test, was first applied to American cattle in Pennsylvania in 1892. From there the practice was soon taken up by dairy farmers across the country. It revealed an alarming rate of bovine tuberculosis in U.S. dairy herds, and marked the start of a long struggle to wipe out the disease. Sick cattle were removed from dairy barns, and their infected milk no longer reached the market. Within a short time there was a noticeable drop in the bovine tuberculosis rate in humans.

The most important new means of preventing the spread of disease by milk was pasteurization.

Pasteurization was named for Louis Pasteur, the French chemist who developed the process. In the 1850s and

1860s Pasteur studied beer, wine, and milk, trying to find out what made these liquids turn sour and spoil. He found that harmful bacteria were responsible. Seeking a way to control the bacteria, Pasteur experimented with heat and discovered that heating wine for a few minutes to a temperature of between 140° and 158° Fahrenheit kept it from souring.

Scientists soon realized that the pasteurization process could also be applied to heating milk. Heating it for thirty minutes or so not only controlled the bacteria that caused the milk to turn sour, but also destroyed most of the disease-carrying bacteria in it. For the first time, the spread of bovine tuberculosis and other diseases could be prevented.

The idea of pasteurizing milk came to America in the 1880s, and was called milk sterilization at first. One doctor said, "I have discovered conclusively that feeding infants sterilized milk instead of raw milk greatly reduces the number of cases of diarrhea."

The long heating process was not completely effective, however. A few dangerous bacteria survived it, and it often gave the milk a boiled taste, making it unacceptable to consumers. Then, in 1891, a German scientist developed a new "flash" method of pasteurization. In it, the milk was heated to a temperature of 184° Fahrenheit for just thirty seconds. This rapid method killed almost all the disease germs in the milk without spoiling its flavor.

Between 1890 and 1900, many pasteurizing machines were invented in Europe and America. The earliest were simply tanks in which large batches of raw milk could be heated by steam or hot water. Later, more elaborate machines were designed that did the job more quickly and efficiently. They consisted of two parts, a heater and a cooler. First the milk flowed in thin sheets over a heated metal surface that raised its temperature to 184° Fahrenheit for anywhere from thirty seconds to a minute. Then it flowed rapidly into a cooler, where the temperature was lowered to 50° before the milk was piped into cans or bottles.

The first milk plant in the United States to install a pasteurizer was the Sheffield Farms Dairy in Bloomville, New Jersey, which imported a German-made machine in 1891. The following year milk pasteurization was demonstrated at the huge Columbian Exposition in Chicago, which celebrated the four hundredth anniversary of Columbus' discovery of America.

Commercial milk pasteurization was introduced in Baltimore in 1893 and in Cincinnati in 1894. New York followed in 1898, Philadelphia in 1899, and St. Louis in 1900.

Despite its obvious advantages, not everyone was in

favor of pasteurization. Many dairymen wanted to avoid the cost of new machinery and claimed the process was unnecessary. Others opposed it for health reasons. They feared that dairy farmers would rely too much on pasteurization to keep their milk safe and let their barns and equipment get dirty. Some even thought that children would be better off drinking the "live" bacteria in raw milk than the "dead" bacteria in pasteurized milk.

Instead of pasteurized milk, many of its opponents favored the use of certified milk. Certified milk was milk whose production was strictly controlled at every stage, from cow to market. Physicians at the Harvard Medical School first developed a plan for certified milk in 1891.

Dairy farmers who followed the Harvard plan agreed to allow their cows to be examined regularly by a team of doctors. The doctors made sure the animals were free of disease. They also inspected the entire physical layout of the farm—barns, land, and water supply—for cleanliness. Other inspectors watched over all aspects of getting the milk to the consumer: collecting and handling procedures, transportation and packaging, and finally delivery. Only if all these safeguards were observed could the milk be labeled "Certified."

This was an expensive process, one that involved the services of chemists, bacteriologists, and veterinarians. As a result, certified milk was not usually available to the general public. In most places it was dispensed by doctors to infants and special patients only.

Meanwhile, the arguments for and against pasteurization continued, and the infant mortality rate remained high, especially in large cities like New York and Chicago. This situation might have lasted for a long time if a strong new supporter of pasteurization hadn't made his appearance in 1893. His name was Nathan Straus, and for the next twenty years he fought an often lonely battle to win acceptance for pasteurization throughout the United States.

6

The Battle for Pasteurization

Nathan Straus, the man who fought for pasteurization, was born in Germany in 1848. His father, Lazarus, emigrated to America in 1854, and Nathan, his mother, and two brothers joined him two years later.

The Straus family spent nine years in a small town in Georgia, where Nathan attended a log-cabin school. After the Civil War ended in 1865, the family moved to New York City, and Mr. Straus started an importing business, L. Straus and Sons. Nathan and his older brother, Isidor, helped their father in the business until 1874, when they left to take jobs with R. H. Macy and Company, already one of New York's well-known department stores. The Straus brothers became partners in Macy's in 1888, and acquired complete ownership of the store in 1896.

From boyhood on Nathan had a good business sense, but he was even more interested in people and their needs. At Macy's he was responsible for providing the store's employees with a low-cost lunchroom and medical care. During the recession winter of 1892–93, he distributed a million and a half buckets of coal to New York's poor. The following winter he established lodging houses that provided a bed and breakfast to homeless men and women for a nickel a night. And starting in 1893 he launched what became a twenty-year campaign for the pasteurization of milk.

Straus had read of Pasteur's work and the advantages of pasteurized milk. He had also heard the arguments against pasteurization by the backers of certified milk. But he knew that ninety-seven out of every thousand children born in New York City died before they reached the age of five. He suspected that impure, unpasteurized milk was one of the chief causes of this high mortality rate, and he decided to do something about it.

The death rate rose in the hot summer months when foods, including milk, were more likely to sour or spoil. So in June 1893, Straus opened a pasteurized-milk depot on the East Third Street pier in a crowded neighborhood of New York City. At the depot mothers could buy safe, pure milk for their babies at a low price: four cents a quart, two cents a pint. For those who found even these prices too high, Straus provided books of free coupons that were handed out by doctors and charitable agencies.

Four children on the sidewalk in front of a grocery store in a New York City slum district, circa 1890. Note milk can at right. Photo by Jacob A. Riis.

The depot dispensed more than just milk. Next to the pasteurizing and bottling plant Straus put up a large, canvas-topped tent filled with benches and tables. There the depot's customers could rest for a while and enjoy the cool river breeze. A doctor and nurse were always on hand to give free medical examinations to children and advice on hygiene to their mothers.

Word of the depot quickly spread, and more and more people used it as the summer wore on. Many came for a new supply of milk every day. They had no means of refrigeration, and milk rarely stayed fresh for more than twenty-four hours in hot summer weather. The depot remained open until November 1893, and distributed more than 34,000 bottles of pasteurized milk that first year.

Straus was so encouraged by the depot's success that the following year he opened five more in other districts of New York City. The six depots distributed more than 300,000 bottles of pasteurized milk in the summer months of 1894.

That fall Straus summed up his experiences with the depots in a magazine article. "Here in New York," he wrote, "the lives of thousands of children are sacrificed every summer, simply because they are fed with impure milk." By contrast, he said, the milk for his depots came from cows that had been examined by veterinarians from the New York Board of Health. The milk was shipped to the city in iced railroad cars and kept on ice until it was pasteurized.

During the pasteurizing process, the milk was exposed for twenty minutes to a temperature of 145° to 167° Fahrenheit. Straus declared that heating the milk for a longer period of time killed even more disease-carrying bacteria than the flash method of pasteurization.

In the next few years Straus opened six more depots in New York, bringing the total to twelve. To convince people that pasteurized milk tasted as good as regular milk, he set up milk stands in parks throughout the city, including Central Park. At the stands people could sample sweet pasteurized milk for a penny a glass.

Straus made no money from operating the depots and stands. As he wrote, "The work is one in which the only possible gain is that of human lives." When Straus spent more in a year on his charitable activities than his interest in Macy's and his other holdings brought in, his devoted brother Isidor made up the difference.

In 1895 Straus began a national campaign on behalf of pasteurized milk. He wrote letters to the mayors of the largest cities in the United States, offering to help establish milk depots in their cities or anywhere else he was asked.

An incident that occurred at a children's home in New York City gave Straus fresh proof of the effectiveness of pasteurization. Orphans and homeless children lived

The pasteurized milk stand in City Hall Park, New York, 1906. Photograph by Byron.

in the home, which was located on Randall's Island in the East River. Between 1895 and 1897 the children were fed what was considered to be safe raw milk from a herd of cows pastured right on the island. Still the death rate among the children from tuberculosis and other diseases was extremely high. Of 3,609 children who were being cared for in the home during those years, 1,509 died.

Nathan Straus was upset when he heard this. Acting quickly, he erected a pasteurization plant on the island in 1898. In one year, without any other changes in the children's diet or hygiene, the mortality rate at the home dropped from 42% of the population to 28%. It continued to drop in the following years, and Straus publicized the good news in articles and speeches. It showed, he said, how important pasteurized milk was to the health of children.

Straus's efforts gradually began to bear fruit. By the early 1900s milk depots patterned on those in New York had been established in such cities as Boston, Philadelphia, Baltimore, Pittsburgh, Cleveland, Chicago, and St. Louis. But Straus still wasn't satisfied. Although pasteurized milk was available in more places than ever before, dairymen and other opponents continued to block all attempts to outlaw the sale of raw milk.

Their opposition did not sway Straus. Instead it strengthened his conviction. He argued that towns and cities had a duty to supply their inhabitants—especially the children—with safe milk, just as they had a duty to supply them with safe water. And he claimed that no amount of inspection, either on the farm, in the dairy, or along the road, could guarantee that raw milk would be free of disease-carrying germs. Only pasteurization could do that.

In the spring of 1907 Straus joined others in New York in urging that an ordinance be passed requiring the pasteurization of all milk sold in the city. Speaking at a mass meeting, Straus said: "The reckless use of raw, unpasteurized milk is little short of a national crime, for which we are paying heavily in ill health, disease, and death."

Straus and his followers were bitterly opposed by many milk distributors in New York, and by physicians and others who promoted the idea of "clean raw milk." Supporting them was the city's Health Department, which insisted that additional inspections of cattle and dairies were the answer. Aided by some important politicians, the opponents of pasteurization defeated the ordinance in May 1907.

Despite this setback Straus continued his campaign, and later in 1907 he received fresh backing from the federal government. President Theodore Roosevelt ordered the Public Health Service to make a thorough study of the milk problem. The Service assembled a panel of twenty experts who investigated the matter from all angles and issued a report early in 1908.

The experts agreed with Straus that raw milk was dangerous and affirmed that pasteurization did not change the chemical composition of milk or affect its taste, digestibility, or nutritive qualities. They summed up their findings by saying, "Pasteurization prevents much sickness and saves many lives."

An inspector from the New York City Department of Health examines a wagonload of milk destined for the city. Photo taken circa 1900.

Following the government report, the New York City Milk Committee tested the comparative value of pasteurized and "clean raw milk." In December 1908, the Committee, which had started out in favor of raw milk, declared itself in favor of pasteurization instead.

Bolstered by the Committee's findings, Nathan Straus appeared before New York City's Board of Aldermen in the spring of 1909. Once again he urged that the city pass an ordinance requiring that all milk be pasteurized. The forces lined up against pasteurization were still strong, however. They argued their case before the Board of Aldermen and persuaded its members to reject Straus's pleas for an ordinance.

Straus's efforts were meeting with more success elsewhere. In August 1908 Chicago became the first U.S. city to require the pasteurization of its milk supply. As of January 1909, all milk sold in Chicago had to be pasteurized, unless it came from cows that had been tuberculin tested within a year and proved to be free of tuberculosis.

Like their counterparts in New York, milk producers and some state officials in Illinois attacked the Chicago ordinance. Nathan Straus wrote an emotional letter to the governor of Illinois saying that if the ordinance were repealed it would be the same as "putting babies in coffins and tearing the hearts of their mothers."

The opponents of the Chicago ordinance retreated

for the moment, but they pressed their attack again in 1910. This time they brought their case to the courts, charging among other things that the pasteurization requirement interfered with free trade.

Straus and his Chicago supporters mounted a new letter-writing campaign, but the courts ignored it and repealed the ordinance. Now the fight for pasteurization in Chicago would have to be waged all over again.

Meanwhile, Straus was cheered by developments on other fronts. In 1910 the Health Department of New York City reversed its previous position and advised the public that all milk for drinking should be either boiled or pasteurized. Then, in 1911, the National Commission on Milk Standards reported that "In the case of all milk not either certified or inspected, pasteurization should be compulsory." Also in 1911 the American Medical Association warned that milk for human consumption must come from tuberculin-tested cows, "or it must be pasteurized."

A movement in favor of pasteurization began to sweep the country. In 1912 Chicago opened discussions about a new citywide ordinance. Nathan Straus wired the Chicago Board of Aldermen: "The ordinance for which you are fighting means lives of babies saved; its defeat means babies killed. Can Chicago hesitate between these alternatives?" The second pasteurization ordinance was adopted by a wide margin.

Back in New York City, the Health Department announced that after January 1, 1912, all milk sold in the city would have to be pasteurized. Milk distributors protested that this ruling would create a hardship for them. They obtained first a delay, and then enough changes in the law so that most milk could still be sold in its raw state.

After an epidemic of typhoid fever hit New York in the fall of 1913, though, the Health Department returned to its original rules. By the summer of 1914, 50% of New York City's milk supply was being pasteurized; and by the fall of that year, 95%.

Philadelphia established compulsory pasteurization in 1914 and other localities followed suit. By 1917 pasteurization was required in forty-six of the fifty-two largest cities in the United States, including Boston, Cleveland, St. Louis, Milwaukee, Denver, Los Angeles, San Francisco, and Seattle. Now there was no longer an urgent need for pasteurized-milk depots, and they gradually shut down.

Nathan Straus had often said, "Humanity is my kin; to save the babies is my religion." The enforcement of compulsory pasteurization laws across the country proved the worth of his twenty-year-long struggle. The death rate of children under five dropped dramatically, and bovine tuberculosis in humans was virtually wiped out.

In 1923 Straus was chosen by popular vote as the

Nathan Straus. Photo by Pach Bros.

citizen who had done the most for the public welfare during the twenty-five years that Greater New York City had existed. In 1930 the National Institute of Social Services awarded him a gold medal "in recognition of the widespread social service he has rendered on behalf of humanity." After his death in 1931, *The American Jewish Year Book* described Straus as "a man of exalted spirituality and firm convictions of righteousness in public and private affairs . . . with a heart overflowing with human sympathy and understanding."

By then the controversies that had surrounded pasteurization had largely been forgotten. Most people now took pasteurized milk and its benefits for granted, and thought that all questions concerning the safety of milk had been answered.

7

The Rotolactor

While Nathan Straus was still waging his battle for pasteurization, dairy farmers across the country were working hard to improve the condition of their milk cattle.

On many farms the cows now lived in clean stables that were well lighted and ventilated. The animals received only wholesome feed, and veterinarians examined them regularly for tuberculosis and other diseases. All utensils used in the milking process were sterilized daily in boiling water.

Farmers shipped their milk to dairies in tightly sealed cans so that there was less chance of bacteria getting into the milk. The cans rode in refrigerated railroad cars that kept the milk from turning sour. In the dairies, wooden floors and walls gave way to tiled surfaces that could be washed down easily and kept spotlessly clean.

Before pasteurization won general acceptance, a national commission tried to establish various grades for milk. The grades were based on the number of harmless bacteria the milk contained. Even if the milk was pasteurized, it was not possible to kill all the bacteria in the liquid.

According to the commission's recommendations, Grade A milk for infants and children had to be either pasteurized or certified and could contain no more than 50,000 bacteria per cubic centimeter. Grade B milk, used by adults and in cooking, had no specific limit on bacteria; the commission simply said the number should not be "excessive." No limit at all was recommended for Grade C milk, which was intended only for cooking.

 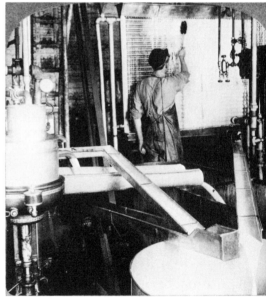

Four scenes in up-to-date dairies of the early 1900s. Left: The pasteurizing equipment. Right: Milk passing over the refrigerating pipes.

It was assumed that any dangerous bacteria in Grade C milk would be killed during the cooking process.

New York City was the first to adopt the new grading system, and other cities and regions followed its example. By 1920 almost every city in America with a population of over 100,000 required both the grading and pasteurization of milk, and most milk sold in those communities was now Grade A.

There were improvements in the pasteurization process itself. In the early 1900s most milk was still being pasteurized by the "flash" method, in which it was heated

Left: Milk bottles leaving the purifying heat of the sterilizer.
Right: Automatic machine for filling and capping bottles of milk.

to 184° Fahrenheit for just a few seconds and then rapidly cooled. However, scientists discovered that while the flash method killed most harmful bacteria, some remained alive and could cause disease.

In 1912, the National Milk Commission urged that, to be on the safe side, dairymen switch to the holding method of pasteurization. This was the method Nathan Straus had used at his milk depots. In it, the milk was held at a temperature of 145° to 167° for at least twenty minutes. Such a high, sustained temperature killed any tuberculosis bacteria that might be in the milk, along with other disease-carrying germs.

The holding method of pasteurization gradually went into effect throughout the United States. It remained the most widely used method until the 1940s, when a more foolproof type of flash pasteurization was developed.

Along with improvements in pasteurization came new developments in the bottling, packaging, and delivery of milk. At the beginning of the twentieth century most milk was still being bottled by hand, and most of the returned bottles were still being washed by hand, too. By the 1920s, though, many dairies were equipped with high-speed machines that could fill, cap, and case five thousand bottles an hour. Inventors had also perfected automatic bottle-washing machines that washed up to one thousand bottles an hour.

Broken and chipped bottles were a problem that had to be watched for carefully. Improved handling led to an average bottle life of thirty-five trips in the 1930s, up from an average of twenty trips in 1915.

Packagers experimented with waxed-paper containers for milk in the 1930s, claiming that they were more economical and more sanitary than bottles. World War II restrictions on paper slowed the development of milk cartons, but they came into widespread use after the war. Today almost all pints and quarts of milk are sold in tightly sealed paper containers.

Before World War II more than 80% of America's milk supply was still being delivered directly to people's homes by wagon or truck. Distributors often painted their vehicles white to suggest to customers that the milk they transported was pure.

Gas rationing during the war helped to hasten the end of home delivery. For the first time, people became accustomed to buying their milk in grocery stores and supermarkets.

While most of the nation's milk supply was now pasteurized, certified milk continued to be available in many places before and after World War II. To help ensure an absolutely pure product, certified-milk dairymen devised some unusual milking methods. One of the most unusual was the Rotolactor, invented by the Walker-Gordon Certified Milk Dairy of New Jersey and dis-

Milk wagon in Cincinnati, Ohio, 1939. Photo by John Vachon.

played to the public at the New York World's Fair of 1939–40.

Called the "cow merry-go-round," the Rotolactor was a rotating circular platform on which fifty stalls were constructed. Each stall was large enough to accommodate one cow facing the center. As the Rotolactor slowly revolved, it could handle the milking of three hundred cows per hour.

Twice a day the 1,650 cows on the Walker-Gordon farm were released from their barns and proceeded single file down a covered alleyway to the washroom. There they were bathed with warm water before moving on to the air-conditioned, dust-free Rotolactor area.

As each cow in turn approached the rotating platform, a vacant stall appeared and she stepped into it. A pair of metal bars, called stanchions, automatically dropped down to hold her in place.

The cow rode to a station along the route where a milker washed her udder with a clean cloth. Then the milker attached a milking machine to the cow. The machine was mounted on the platform by her stall, and was sterilized between uses. Once the machine was attached, the cow rode on and the milker turned his attention to the next animal.

The Rotolactor made a complete revolution in ten minutes, just the time it took to finish milking the cow. The milk was drawn through sterilized, airtight tubes to individual sealed glass containers. From them it flowed into an automatic weighing and recording machine before being bottled.

At the end of the revolution, the cow found herself facing an open runway. The milking machine was removed, and the stanchions holding the cow were raised. She stepped off the platform, walked down the runway underneath the Rotolactor, and returned to the barn, where her feed was waiting.

The cow's stall on the platform was immediately claimed by another animal and the milking process was repeated. It took approximately six hours to milk all the cows on

New Jersey schoolchildren visiting the Rotolactor at the Walker-Gordon Certified Milk Dairy.

the Walker-Gordon farm. The only thing the "cow merry-go-round" lacked was music.

People watching the Rotolactor in action at the New York World's Fair thought they were getting a glimpse of how milking would be done in the future. And in many respects they were right. For although few regular dairies ever adopted the Rotolactor itself, they did copy many of the sanitary techniques associated with it.

Because of these improved sanitation methods, people in the postwar United States had more confidence in the safety and purity of milk than ever before. Then, suddenly and unexpectedly, a new danger to milk loomed on the international scene. It was one of the frightening, unforeseen consequences of the atomic bomb and the arms race that followed.

8

Danger from the Sky

The United States dropped atomic bombs on Hiroshima and Nagasaki, Japan, in August 1945, and soon afterward World War II came to an end. Almost immediately the Western powers, led by the United States, and the Eastern bloc, led by the Soviet Union, began an arms race to develop and perfect atomic weapons. The United States had a monopoly until 1949, when the Soviet Union exploded its first atomic bomb.

Great Britain followed with an atomic bomb of its own in 1952. That same year the United States startled the world by exploding an even more powerful hydrogen bomb at its test site in the South Pacific. A year later, in 1953, the Soviet Union caught up when it exploded a hydrogen bomb at a test site in Siberia.

Every explosion of a nuclear bomb produces thousands of particles of radioactive material. The particles are so tiny that they cannot be seen under even the most powerful microscope.

*Smoke billows up over Nagasaki, Japan, after an atomic bomb is
dropped on the city, August 9, 1945.*

Hot, churning gases lift the particles high into the atmosphere, and strong winds carry them far and wide. Eventually they fall to earth with rain and snow, landing in rivers and lakes, on the leaves of trees and plants, and in the soil. This is what is commonly known as atomic fallout.

Most of the fallout presents no health hazards because it breaks down rapidly and becomes harmless. But some of the fallout retains its radioactivity for longer periods of time. If it is absorbed by grass and other plants that are eaten by cows, it will appear later on in the cow's milk. Pasteurization does not affect radioactive fallout, which will still be in the milk when a child or adult drinks it.

Radiation comes at people from many different sources—cosmic rays from outer space, X rays in doctors' offices, television sets—but the levels are usually so low that they do no lasting harm to the body's cells. However, people began to be alarmed in the late 1940s and the 1950s when they realized that radiation levels in milk and other foods were rising noticeably because of the atomic test explosions.

The two types of atomic radiation detected most often in milk were strontium 90 and iodine 131.

Strontium 90, like calcium, accumulates in bones and is especially dangerous to young children whose bones are still being formed. Scientists warned that high levels of strontium 90 in the human body might lead to cancer, leukemia, or premature aging, and be transmitted through the genes to future generations.

Although it decays more rapidly than strontium 90, iodine 131 can also reach the table in foods like milk. It accumulates in the thyroid gland, where it may eventually produce a life-threatening cancer. Children are more likely to be affected by iodine 131 than adults.

Testing of atomic weapons continued at a rapid rate as the 1950s wore on. Scientists estimated that between 1945 and 1958, nuclear bombs with a total energy equal to more than eight thousand Hiroshima-type bombs were tested by the United States, Great Britain, and the Soviet Union. Many of these were exploded in the atmosphere, creating huge amounts of fallout. By late 1958 over two hundred pounds of strontium 90 had been produced in atomic explosions and had spread worldwide.

A sampling of milk in forty-eight U.S. and Canadian cities found that the average strontium 90 content was at least two times greater in mid-1958 than it had been in 1957. Laboratory tests in 1957–58 showed that the bones of American children under four contained three times as many units of strontium 90 as they had in 1954–55.

When Americans heard these figures, they reacted with shock and alarm. The Atomic Energy Commission

(AEC)—the forerunner of the present Nuclear Regulatory Commission—tried to reassure them by saying that the increased amounts of strontium 90 in milk and other foods were still far below the danger level.

Not everyone agreed with the government's view of the situation. For example, a conference of scientists in 1958 took a very different stand. In a statement issued at the end of the conference, the scientists said: "The atomic bomb tests produce a definite health hazard that will claim a significant number of victims in present and future generations."

Later in 1958 the Western powers and the Soviet Union met in Geneva, Switzerland, to discuss a nuclear test ban treaty. The United States, speaking for the West, argued that an international system of inspection had to be developed before testing could stop. The Soviet Union countered by proposing an immediate ban on nuclear weapons, with the possibility that some sort of inspection system would be established later.

While the discussions continued, both sides stepped up the pace of testing, and public protests mounted. From New York to London to Paris, people marched in nuclear disarmament demonstrations. They carried banners that read: "Ban the Bomb," "Make the Future Safe for Our Children," and "The Only 'Safe' Dose of Radiation Is No Dose At All!"

*Participants in the 100-mile March for Peace, 1961. Committee for a
Sane Nuclear Policy photo.*

At last, in the autumn of 1958, the three atomic powers agreed to suspend testing for one year. Millions of people all over the world felt a sense of relief, but fallout levels remained high because of all the bombs that had been tested earlier.

Starting in 1959, the U.S. Public Health Service, the Agricultural Research Service, and the Atomic Energy Commission worked to develop a method for removing strontium 90 and other radioactivity from fluid milk. They came up with a complicated process that involved treating the milk with citric acid and electrically charged resins. Together these removed more than 95% of the radioactivity in the milk, but there were problems with the process. If it wasn't properly conducted, it could significantly increase the number of bacteria in the milk. It would also be expensive, and might raise the price of milk beyond what many consumers could afford to pay.

Scientists suggested other steps that could be taken in case the level of nuclear fallout rose dramatically in a particular region. They recommended that dairy cattle be fed no fresh forage until the emergency passed. And they urged that all supplies of liquid milk be imported from uncontaminated areas.

In 1959 the atomic powers extended the temporary ban on tests while discussions on a permanent-test-ban treaty continued. Many people were still worried about the high fallout levels in milk, but the Consumers' Union sounded a more positive note. "Because of its food value," the Union said in an article, "it would be as foolish to stop drinking milk as it would be to refuse an X-ray examination for a broken limb." In other words, even though the milk, like the X ray, might contain radiation, in neither case was it a large enough amount to be harmful.

The ban on atomic tests remained in effect until 1961, when the Soviet Union broke it, claiming that not enough progress was being made in the talks. The United States followed suit with new bomb tests of its own in the spring of 1962. As a consequence, the amounts of strontium 90 and iodine 131 in milk rose to new heights in the summer and fall of 1962.

Health officials in Salt Lake City, Utah, detected so much iodine 131 in the city's milk supply that they issued a warning. Until the iodine 131 level went down, they urged pregnant women, mothers who were breast-feeding their babies, and all young children to drink only evaporated milk or powdered milk. Since iodine 131 breaks down rapidly, and it took an average of two months for evaporated and powdered milk to reach consumers, those forms of milk were considered safe.

Despite such measures, it was apparent that fallout from atomic tests had already done lasting damage. In early 1963 the Federal Radiation Council estimated that during the next seventy years, as many as two thousand

Young demonstrators protest the resumption of atomic testing in the atmosphere, 1962. Committee for a Sane Nuclear Policy photo.

more cases of leukemia might occur in the United States because of the nuclear testing conducted through 1962. As many as fifteen thousand more children might be born with physical or mental defects because of radiation damage done to their parents. Some scientists thought the Council's figures were far too low.

The United States, Great Britain, and the Soviet Union finally signed a permanent-test-ban treaty in the summer of 1963. It outlawed all nuclear tests in the atmosphere, in outer space, and under water.

France, which had exploded its first atomic bomb in 1960, did not sign the treaty. Nor did China and India, both of which later developed atomic bombs and tested them in the atmosphere. The United States, Great Britain, and the Soviet Union have abided by the treaty, however. As a result, the amount of fallout from nuclear explosions has steadily dwindled.

There remains the danger of an accidental release of radioactive materials from a uranium mine or a nuclear power plant, like the disaster that occurred in the Soviet Union in the spring of 1986. But as long as the atomic powers refrain from nuclear tests in the atmosphere, the levels of strontium 90 and other radioactive materials will probably remain low. Still, people throughout the world aren't likely to forget the alarm they felt in the 1950s and 1960s when they first realized how easily our environment—and one of our most basic foods—could be poisoned.

Meanwhile, new threats to milk have made their appearance in the 1970s and 1980s. This time they haven't come from the sky, but from right here on earth.

9

Poisoned Feed, Poisoned Milk

In the fall of 1973 many dairy farmers in Michigan noticed that their cows lacked energy and had lost their appetites. Some animals refused to eat altogether. Veterinarians who were called in to examine the cows couldn't determine what was wrong with them. Their symptoms didn't point to any known disease.

The sick animals continued to lose weight, and milk production dropped. By January 1974 some cows were too weak to stand. Their once-glossy coats had become dull, and the skin on their necks and shoulders was as wrinkled as an elephant's hide. Many of those that were pregnant gave birth to dead calves.

The Michigan dairy farmers involved began to grow frantic. It was costing them more to care for their sick animals than they were getting from the sale of milk. The farmers suspected that there might be something wrong with the protein-enriched feed they'd been giving their cows. The feed was supposed to contain Nutri-

Purebred Holstein cattle being fed enriched silage.

master, a trade name for magnesium oxide. This harmless substance helped a cow's digestion and thus increased her milk output.

Several of the farmers sent feed samples to various agricultural research stations for testing. Scientists at the stations thought chemical pest killers might have gotten into the feed, but all their tests proved negative.

79

Meanwhile, more and more cattle showed symptoms of the mysterious disease.

At last, in the spring of 1974, scientists at a Department of Agriculture research center in Maryland performed new tests on the feed and discovered what was causing all the trouble. Instead of magnesium oxide, the feed contained large amounts of polybrominated biphenyl—PBB for short.

PBB is a substance intended to help prevent fabrics and plastics from catching fire. It is not intended to be consumed internally. If animals or people swallow small quantities of PBB over a period of time, it accumulates in their fatty tissue and livers. Serious health problems can result. When autopsies were performed on some of the Michigan cattle that had died, it was found that their livers were greatly enlarged.

Since PBB accumulated in fat, it would eventually show up in the milk of cows that had swallowed it. This would happen slowly, and at a steadily decreasing rate if the cow took in no more PBB. While the process was going on, though, the cow's milk would contain traces of PBB. And it would be absorbed into the tissues of the people who drank it.

As soon as the cause of the problem was located, sale of magnesium-enriched feed was temporarily halted in Michigan. At the same time, investigators sought to find out where and how PBB had gotten into the feed to begin with.

The trail led first to Farm Bureau Services, which operated the largest agricultural feed plant in Michigan, and then to the Michigan Chemical Corporation. The chemical firm supplied Nutrimaster to Farm Bureau Services. It also manufactured Firemaster, a fire retardant containing PBB.

Both substances had a white, crumbly appearance and both were often packed for sale in fifty-pound brown-paper sacks. Apparently someone at Michigan Chemical had confused the two and shipped a large amount of Firemaster to Farm Bureau Services by mistake. There it was routinely mixed into cattle feed that was sold to hundreds of dairy farmers throughout Michigan.

Once the source of the mix-up had been pinpointed, further poisoning could be halted. But no one knew how much damage had already been done. Nor was there any known cure for the thousands of cattle that had been affected.

Starting in May 1974 the Michigan Department of Agriculture tested the bulk milk tanks in dairies around the state for evidence of PBB. The U.S. Food and Drug Administration had set a safety level of one part per million of PBB in milk, measured in the fat content. When the inspectors found higher levels of PBB than that, they forbade sale of the milk and tracked down the dairy farmers who had supplied it. The farmers were served with quarantine notices and told they could no longer send their milk to market.

In an attempt to reassure the public, the Michigan Department of Agriculture issued a statement. It said: "Only a very few of the state's 8,000 Grade A dairy farms are involved, and the feed and chemical in question have been recalled. Also, milk from contaminated herds has been removed from the market. Thus, there is little need for concern about public milk supplies."

In the summer of 1974 the Michigan state legislature authorized the state's Department of Agriculture to find a disposal site for severely poisoned cows. After a state-wide search, a site for the burial in northern Michigan's Kalkaska County was approved. No one lived within two miles of the place, which was surrounded by deep pine woods. It was also three miles from the nearest river, so there was little chance of PBB getting into the water supply.

Starting in late summer, sick cows by the hundreds were trucked to Kalkaska. Many owners, who loved their animals, followed in cars to make sure the slaughter was done humanely.

Some of the cows died in the trucks before they ever reached Kalkaska. Others were so weak when they arrived that they had to be dragged to the burial pit. Some-

Sick and dying cows being trucked to Kalkaska.

times their watching owners helped to urge the animals along. They wanted to see their suffering come to an end at last. "Move on, Janie," they would say, or "Keep going, Brownie." They spoke in the same calm, soothing tones they had used with the animals at milking time.

At the edge of the pit, a veterinarian injected a powerful muscle relaxant into the cow's veins. She quickly fell unconscious, and then the veterinarian shot her through the brain. Her corpse was lifted on a crane and buried in a trench under thick layers of sand, clay, and topsoil.

At first the mass grave was meant to hold no more than five thousand animals. But as increasing numbers of cows showed symptoms of PBB poisoning, the grave was expanded. Eventually more than twenty-five thousand infected cows would be trucked to Kalkaska.

The burial site at Kalkaska.

In the meantime, the Food and Drug Administration decided its original safety level of one part per million of PBB in milk was too high. In the fall of 1974 it lowered it to 0.3 parts per million. This led to more milk being rejected and more dairy farms being quarantined.

In the winter of 1974–75 symptoms of PBB poisoning started to appear in members of farm families who had drunk the milk and eaten the meat of infected animals. Usually healthy men and women experienced fierce headaches, stomach upsets, skin eruptions, and sudden weight loss. Children suffered from aching limbs and colds that lasted for weeks. Some people were troubled by poor coordination and a failure to judge distances. One farmer said he was "becoming as clumsy as my poor sick cows."

Urban residents complained of mysterious ailments, too. One fourteen-year-old Detroit athlete, who had always drunk a lot of milk, was hit especially hard. Between early November and Christmas 1974 he lost thirty pounds for no apparent reason, his hair began to fall out, and his coordination became uncertain. Doctors familiar with the PBB poisoning of cattle said that this boy displayed the exact same symptoms.

In 1976 medical experts in Michigan launched the first large-scale studies of the effects of PBB on human health. In one study, over one thousand members of farm families were given extensive tests. A third of them suffered from ailments that seemed to be related to PBB.

One family's situation was especially revealing. Of five children in the family, four showed symptoms of PBB poisoning: muscle aches, frequent stomach upsets, general weakness. Only one four-year-old girl appeared to be completely healthy. When she was a baby, she had been a poor eater, so her mother had given her powdered milk rather than milk from the family's herd of cows.

In another study, the Michigan Department of Public Health took breast-milk samples from 108 women who gave birth in Michigan hospitals during August and September 1976. All the women bought milk and other dairy foods in urban supermarkets. The results of the study were a shock. Ninety-six percent of the women had detectable levels of PBB in their milk, and some of them had more than four times the level acceptable for cow's milk.

The Department of Public Health emphasized that the amounts of PBB found in the Michigan mothers had not caused the women any apparent harm. But no one could be sure what long-term effects the PBB might have on the mothers—and their babies.

After reports on these studies were published, public

pressure mounted anew for a reduction of the PBB tolerance levels in milk and meat. As a result, the Michigan State Senate voted to lower the level from 0.3 parts per million to 0.02 parts per million. In another law, the state guaranteed loans at little or no interest to dairy farmers whose cattle failed to meet the stricter standards. It also urged research scientists to find a way to flush PBB residues out of animal and human tissues.

Meanwhile, all production of PBB had ceased, not only in Michigan but throughout the country. This happened after the Environmental Protection Agency ruled that PBB's effectiveness as a fire retardant was far outweighed by its potential to harm those who produced, handled, and used it.

The danger from PBB was over, at least for the moment. But as one scientist pointed out, "We won't be able to close the books on the Michigan case until we see what happens to all the people who were affected. And we won't know that until at least twenty years from now."

Fortunately, the milk people consume is safe in most parts of the United States today. Sanitation standards on farms and in dairy processing plants are higher than ever. To make certain they remain that way, the U.S. Public Health Service requires that dairy farms be inspected at least twice a year, and milk-processing plants at least four times a year. In many places they're inspected much more frequently. Some states regularly inspect milk-processing plants at least twice a month.

Despite such care, problems with milk safety still crop up—often where they're least expected.

10

The Fight Continues

To avoid contamination, the milk we drink today is rarely exposed to light or air from the time it leaves the cow until we pour it into a glass.

Every morning and evening a typical dairy farmer drives his cows into a spotless milking barn and attaches sterilized tubes to their teats. The tubes are connected to milking machines that send the milk into a stainless steel pipe. The pipe carries the milk directly to a big steel refrigerated tank outside the milking barn.

Once a day a dairy tank truck drives up to the milking barn and pumps out the milk. Samples are taken for possible later examination in the dairy's laboratory. The truck goes on to pick up milk from several other farms and then carries it all to the dairy's processing plant.

Scientists in the laboratory test the truck's load of milk for bacteria. Federal guidelines allow milk that will be pasteurized to contain 300,000 bacteria per milliliter when it reaches the plant. The guidelines assume that

On this present-day dairy farm, before the cow leaves the barn to be milked her udder and flanks are washed with a clean cloth.

all but approximately 20,000 bacteria will be killed in the pasteurizing process, and that none of the remaining bacteria will be harmful to the human body.

The scientists also test the load for the presence of antibiotics. Antibiotics enter milk through the body of a cow that has been given injections of a drug like

COURTESY OF U.S. DEPARTMENT OF AGRICULTURE

Cows are milked by machine at a dairy farm in Wisconsin.

penicillin for the treatment of a disease or infection. Once they get into the milk, the antibiotics can't be removed. So any batch of milk that is found to contain them will have to be dumped, since no antibiotics are permitted in food intended for human consumption.

After the truckload of milk has passed inspection, it is pumped into tall, refrigerated silos. There whirling machines remove any bits of hay or other solid impurities that might have gotten into the milk at the farm. They also separate the butterfat from some of it, leaving the skim milk.

The fat content of the remaining milk is then adjusted so that it can be sold as either low-fat or whole milk, and all of the milk ends up in big tanks, in which it is pasteurized. Most dairies today use the flash method of pasteurization. The milk is heated to a temperature of 170° Fahrenheit and held there for sixteen or so seconds.

Besides pasteurizing milk in the usual fashion, some dairies now are sterilizing it completely. In this process, the milk is heated to a temperature of 280° or 290° Fahrenheit for just three or four seconds, and all bacteria in the liquid are killed.

Because of the complete absence of bacteria, sterile milk can be kept for up to six or eight months, with or without refrigeration. The Army and Navy purchase it for use on military maneuvers and long voyages, and campers and hikers like it also. But sterile milk has its

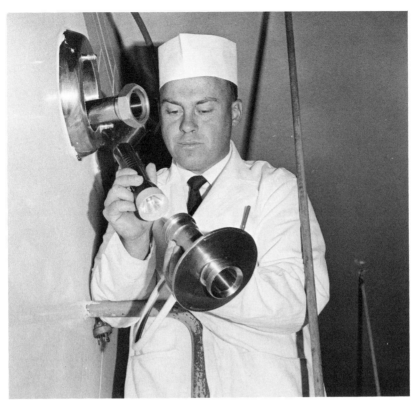

An area supervisor for the U.S. Department of Agriculture disassembles pipelines in a Minneapolis, Minnesota, dairy to make sure they contain no residues that could affect the milk.

drawbacks. The high pasteurizing temperature sometimes affects the lactose sugar, giving the milk a slightly caramel flavor. And it is considerably more expensive than regular milk. These drawbacks will probably keep sterile milk from ever replacing pasteurized milk as the favorite of most consumers.

At the same time the milk is pasteurized, it is also homogenized. The homogenization process has nothing to do with the purity or safety of milk. It prevents the cream in the milk from rising to the top by forcing the liquid through a fine steel mesh and breaking the globules of fat into tiny particles. Homogenization came into widespread use in the 1940s, and today is applied to almost all milk that Americans drink.

Once the milk has been pasteurized and homogenized, pipes carry it into the bottling section of the plant, where it is packaged in plastic jugs and paper cartons. Each container is stamped with an expiration date beyond which the milk cannot be sold. These dates vary somewhat from city to city and state to state, but all are based on the time the milk is expected to remain fresh and sweet. In New York City, for example, milk cannot be sold more than four days after it has been pasteurized. Expiration dates in other places range from five to ten days.

Refrigerated trucks deliver the jugs and cartons of whole milk, low-fat milk, and skim milk to small stores and giant supermarkets. There customers load the containers into their shopping carts, confident that they are buying a safe, pure product. And most of the time they're right.

Accidents can still occur, however. Sometimes milk is delivered in trucks with faulty refrigeration systems

Scientists at the Agricultural Research Center in Beltsville, Maryland, measure the flow rates through a homogenizer. Photo by Jim Strawser.

Shopper in the dairy section of a supermarket. Photo by Fred S. Witte.

that fail to keep the temperature below 40° Fahrenheit. Or stores may leave cases of milk warming on the side-walk or on supermarket shelves. This allows bacteria to grow in the milk, and it's likely to turn sour before the expiration date stamped on the carton.

More serious problems have been linked to the continuing sale of raw, certified milk. Although certified milk is produced today at only two dairies, one in Georgia and the other in California, its sale is permitted in eighteen other states.

Some people believe that raw, certified milk is healthier than pasteurized milk. Like its supporters at the beginning of the century, they claim that raw milk contains important nutrients and enzymes that are lost in the pasteurization process. But wherever certified raw milk is sold, there has been a noticeable increase in childhood sicknesses such as diarrhea that pasteurization all but wiped out.

Reacting to these health problems, citizen groups in many places have urged the federal government to outlaw the sale of raw milk. Meanwhile, local and state health departments are keeping a closer watch on its production and distribution.

Pasteurization doesn't always work perfectly, either. In Illinois in the spring of 1985, there was a mysterious outbreak of salmonella. Hundreds of people came down with the symptoms of the disease—high fever, stomach cramps, vomiting—and no one could figure out why.

Investigators from the Illinois Department of Public Health set out to discover the cause of the outbreak. While they searched, new cases of salmonella were reported in four other states: Iowa, Indiana, Wisconsin, and Michigan.

The investigators finally traced the path of the disease back to a suburban Chicago dairy. There they found that an improperly installed valve had allowed raw milk containing the salmonella bacteria to mix with pasteurized milk.

All the dairy's milk and other products were immediately recalled from stores. But by then more than fifteen thousand people in five states were suffering from salmonella, and two deaths had been linked to the disease.

Incidents like these prove that the fight for pure milk—like the fight for the purity and safety of other consumer items—is an ongoing one.

In the 150 or so years since people first became aware of the health problems connected with impure milk, many individuals have led the struggle for milk safety. From Frank Leslie's exposure of the swill-milk industry to Nathan Straus's one-man battle for pasteurization to the protestors against atomic testing in the atmosphere, these individuals risked their reputations and sometimes their fortunes in order to save lives. And they accomplished a great deal.

The fight is far from over, though. Pasteurization, as we have seen, is not always foolproof. Another poisonous substance like PBB might get into cattle feed and create a health hazard for even more people than were affected in Michigan. Extensive atomic testing may be resumed, or some unforeseen nuclear accident could pollute the atmosphere and threaten the milk supply.

To guard against such things happening, people in the future will have to be as alert to possible dangers as were the Nathan Strauses of the past. Only then will the children of the next century be assured a safe, healthful supply of that essential food—milk.

Bibliography

Bettmann, Otto L. *The Good Old Days—They Were Terrible!* New York: Random House, 1974.

Boorstin, Daniel J. *The Americans: The Democratic Experience.* New York: Random House, 1973.

Braudel, Fernand. *The Structures of Everyday Life: The Limits of the Possible.* New York: Harper & Row, 1982.

Chang, K. C. *Food in Chinese Culture.* New Haven and London: Yale University Press, 1977.

Chen, Edwin. *PBB: An American Tragedy.* Englewood Cliffs, N. J.: Prentice-Hall, Inc., 1979.

Consumer Reports. Series of articles "Fallout in Our Food": "The Milk All of Us Drink, and Fallout," March 1959; "Fallout in Our Milk: A Follow-up Report," February 1960; "Strontium-90 in Milk: Action Needed," January 1962; "Getting the Strontium-90 Out of Milk," February 1962; "More States Act on Iodine-131 in Milk," October 1962; "Fallout in Our Food," April 1963; "Fallout, 1963," September 1963.

Egginton, Joyce. *The Poisoning of Michigan.* New York and London: W. W. Norton & Company, 1980.

Frank Leslie's Illustrated Newspaper. Volumes for the years 1858–59. ("Startling Exposure of the Milk Trade of New York and Brooklyn"— issue of May 8, 1858)

100

Fussell, G. E. *The English Dairy Farmer: 1500–1900*. London: Frank Cass & Co., Ltd., 1966.

Hartley, Dorothy. *Lost Country Life*. New York: Pantheon Books, 1979.

Hartley, Robert M. *An Historical, Scientific, and Practical Essay on Milk as an Article of Human Sustenance*. New York: Jonathan Leavitt, 1842. Reprint. New York: Arno Press, 1977.

Murthy, Gopala Krishna. *Profile of Long-Lived Radionuclides in Milk*. Cincinnati, Ohio: U.S. Department of Health, Education, and Welfare, 1964.

Oski, Frank A., M.D., with John D. Bell. *Don't Drink Your Milk!* Chicago: Wyden Books, 1977.

Proulx, E. Annie, and Lew Nichols. *The Complete Dairy Foods Cookbook*. Emmaus, Pa.: Rodale Press, 1982.

Science News Letter. "Radioactive Milk Cleansed, Peril Eased," March 13, 1965.

Selitzer, Ralph. *The Dairy Industry in America*. New York: Dairy and Ice Cream Field and Books for Industry, 1976.

Straus, Lina Gutherz. *Disease in Milk, the Remedy Pasteurization: The Life Work of Nathan Straus*. 1917. Reprint. New York: Arno Press, 1977.

Straus, Nathan. *Report on the Progress Made in America in the Protection of Child Life Submitted to the Third International Congress for the Protection of Infants, Berlin, September 11–15, 1911*. New York: 1911.

U.S. Department of Agriculture, Agricultural Marketing Service, Dairy Division. *General Instructions for Performing Farm Inspections According to the USDA Recommended Requirements for Milk*. Washington, D.C., U.S. Government Printing Office, 1976.

U.S. Department of Health, Education, and Welfare, Public Health Service, Bureau of Disease Prevention and Environmental Control. *Full-Scale System for the Removal of Radiostrontium from Fluid Milk*. Rockville, Maryland: National Center for Radiological Health, 1967.

U.S. Department of Health, Education, and Welfare, Public Health Service, Food and Drug Administration. *Requirements of Laws and Regu-*

lations Enforced by the U.S. Food and Drug Administration. Washington, D.C.: U.S. Government Printing Office, 1980.

U.S. Public Health Service. *Milk and its Relation to the Public Health.* Washington, D.C.: U.S. Government Printing Office, 1908.

Van Ingen, Philip, M.D., and Paul Emmons Taylor, Editors. *Infant Mortality and Milk Stations.* New York: The New York Milk Committee, 1912.

Index

Numbers in *italics* indicate illustrations.

105